A Gaelic Alphabet

A Gaelic
ALPHABET

A GUIDE TO THE
PRONUNCIATION
OF GAELIC
LETTERS AND WORDS

George McLennan

ARGYLL✠PUBLISHING
Glendaruel Argyll Scotland

© George McLennan

First published 2009
Argyll Publishing
Glendaruel
Argyll PA22 3AE
www.argyllpublishing.com

The author has asserted his moral rights.

**Chuidich Comhairle nan Leabhraichean
am foillsichear le cosgaisean an leabhair seo.**

**British Library Cataloguing-in-Publication Data.
A catalogue record for this book is available from
the British Library.**

ISBN 978 1 906134 33 4

Printing Bell & Bain Ltd, Glasgow

CONTENTS

INTRODUCTION

The Gaelic alphabet is one of the shortest of the European Latin-based alphabets. Its predecessor, the cumbersome Og(h)am alphabet, used in Old Irish from the fourth to the sixth century AD, had twenty 'letters'. These are sets of grooves or notches on a line such as the edge of a gravestone.[1]

The modern Gaelic alphabet has 18 letters; the English alphabet, in contrast, has 26. Gaelic does not have any letters which are not in the English alphabet, but is missing eight which are. These are **j k q v w x y z**. This does not mean that the **sounds** of these letters in English are missing in Gaelic – all languages use letters slightly differently from each other – and Gaelic has sounds for seven of the missing eight. The following words, **J**ura, **K**ilmun, **V**atersay, **W**ick, ta**x**i, **T**yndrum, spelled in the English way, all have their own Gaelic spellings. Only the last letter **z** is not a traditional Gaelic sound, although a version of it is frequently heard in today's Gaelic spellings of words borrowed from English such as **bhàsa** 'vase', **siop** 'zip' etc. So Gaelic simply needs a smaller alphabet to make its sounds; and it is recognised that the English alphabet has unnecessary letters – c/k, x/c(k)s, q/cw as in words like *lax/ lacks* etc. The sounds of English alphabet letters which are missing from Gaelic are made by Gaelic using combinations of letters in various ways.

---

1. Ogam had **q**, **ng** and **z,** which Gaelic does not, but, not surprisingly, doesn't have **p**, which is not an original Gaelic letter. (See under **P**.)

English itself does this, of course. Some letters in the Greek alphabet are missing in the English alphabet – the Greek letter Φ requires the two English letters **ph** (Italian uses just one, **f**) for its sound; English could of course also have used **f**, so **ph** could be regarded as another unnecessary pairing. Gaelic also has **f** and **ph**, but has the excuse that **p** is not an original letter of its alphabet, as mentioned above.

So to pronounce Gaelic words approximately correctly you need to know what the sounds of the letters are, particularly the sounds of combinations of letters. Otherwise you are liable to pronounce the Skye whisky **Tè Bheag** as Tea Bag, which is how many drinkers and those in the wines and spirits trade in England (and possibly elsewhere) pronounce it. This could perhaps be useful as a marketing ploy in some Middle East countries, but might be rather counter-productive elsewhere.

As rough guides to pronunciation I have used common English words and sounds, as they are pronounced in Scotland, rather than international phonetic symbols with which many people may not be familiar.[2] This may not be very scientific but it can be quite helpful. So a more authentic pronunciation of **tè bheag** mentioned above would be *tchay vek*. The only exception to this is that I have made use of *ə*.

This symbol, like an upside-down **e**, is called schwa (or shwa) and is widely used to indicate a neutral vowel in an unaccented syllable as in the English words *infənt* and *randəm*. It is also sometimes found in Gaelic with vowels carrying the stress – monosyllables like **lagh** 'law' for instance. So Gaelic

---

2. The problem with English words, of course, is that the same combination of letters can have different sounds. So although *ow* has been used to illustrate the sound of **clann** (*clown*), the Gaelic sound doesn't bring the lips forward to reflect the *w* as English does. The vowel sound of the English word *noun* is more like the Gaelic.

monadh 'moor' will have its pronunciation illustrated phonetically by *monəgh*.

The important thing to remember always is that Gaelic words are stressed on the first syllable. I have also made considerable use of Scottish placenames and surnames to illustrate particular pronunciations, in the expectation that most people will be familiar with many of them. Fewer may be familiar with Manx (Isle of Man Gaelic) and Welsh, but they provide helpful parallels from different sides of the Celtic language family, so I've cited them occasionally.

An important feature of Gaelic spelling is the 'broad to broad and slender to slender' rule. This means that if a consonant has a broad vowel (**a,o,u**) immediately in front of it, it must be followed immediately by a broad vowel; in the same way a slender vowel (**e,i**) has to be followed up by a slender vowel. So **meatailt** 'metal' is borrowed from English but can't be written in the English way (*metal*) because the **t** has a slender vowel (**e**) on one side and a broad vowel (**a**) on the other. So in the Gaelic form the first **a** doesn't have a sound of its own and is only there because of the spelling rule. This is why Gaelic words often seem to be longer than English ones from which they are borrowed.

In theory a Gaelic spelling *metilt* would not offend against the spelling rule; it would, however, give the wrong sound to the **t** (and the next **t** and **l**) – see under **T** and **L** – and the **e** standing alone is also not quite acceptable (see under **E**). This is why the spelling rule is important; the form *metal* doesn't make clear which of two main Gaelic sounds of the **t** is meant.

Each letter is discussed separately, first the consonants in alphabetical order, except that **H** comes before the others for reasons that will become clear. Combinations of consonants, eg **chd**, are dealt with or referred to under the first letter. The vowels are then done in alphabetical order; groups of vowels, **ai**, **ao**, etc. are dealt with under the first-mentioned letter. Since letters do not usually stand in isolation within a word, but influence each other in various ways, cross-references are made from one letter to another throughout.

There is no doubt that many people who do not know Gaelic well, or at all, have a problem with its pronunciation. An ability to say words reasonably correctly when seeing them in print depends and relies to a great extent on correct spelling. This may seem an outdated idea in this age of mis-spellings and grammatical errors in even quality newspapers and other literature, but unless you have an idea of Gaelic spelling conventions, you may find it harder to identify even modern words borrowed from English; words such as **sutha** for zoo, **faidhle** for file (document), and so on.

This is also the age of texting, with its cavalier approach to spelling. While the use of texting strengthens Gaelic's place in the world of modern communications, it has slightly negative implications for the language. Since brevity is the point of texting, Gaelic uses letters foreign to its alphabet – those mentioned in the first paragraph above. So we find *gl va* (**glè mhath**, 'very good') and *n ju* (**an-diugh**, 'today'). Still, better dubious Gaelic texting than no Gaelic texting at all.

Finally, I have tried to give phonetic pronunciations of what might be termed mainstream Gaelic, although the speech of most Gaelic speakers reflects the influence of their geographic background. There is not really an equivalent in Gaelic of the non-regional accent found in so-called upper class English voices. From time to time, however, I have mentioned a regional pronunciation where I think it might be of interest.

H

Uath – Hawthorn

All letters of the Gaelic alphabet are named after trees or shrubs. Some letters have more than one name, and some words describe more than one letter, so I've given the most widely accepted ones. This is an Old Irish classification and so the names for the letters are not necessarily those of today.

Hawthorn in Gaelic is now **Sgitheach**. Scottish placenames featuring these trees and shrubs use the more modern word, though the older forms **Coll** and **Iogh** are also found; place-names often retain old words and forms.

As with other languages (English **A** is for **a**pple etc.), the plant name begins with the letter that it represents, in order, presumably, to make it easier for people to remember the letters. The exception to this is **uath** for **H** as indicated above, but this is not really surprising since **h** is a breathing rather than a proper letter and was sometimes not used in the past.

Although it does not really have an existence of its own, **H** is a good letter to start with since it plays such an important role in the language. In other words, it rarely stands by itself, but instead is usually found immediately following another consonant – at the beginning, middle or end of a word, often all three, eg **bhàthadh**, 'drowned'. On the rare occasions when it stands by itself, ie not immediately after a consonant, its purpose is usually to prevent elision, for instance **na h-eòin**, 'the birds', and on such occasions it is sounded like an English **h** in '**he**' etc. So in Islay we have **Port na h-Abhainne** (Portnahaven), Port of the River. The word for 'river' is **abhainn** (English *Avon*, of which there are several, a couple of them in Scotland), and the **h** in front of it on this occasion simply makes it easier to say.

There are quite a number of placenames in Gaelic starting with **h** but they are mostly borrowings from Old Norse or pre-Gaelic; **Hiort** or **Hirt** (St Kilda), **Hearach** (a native of Harris) and **Hallaig** (on Raasay), the subject of a celebrated poem by Sorley MacLean, are three of the better known.

As a result most Gaelic dictionaries do not have any original Gaelic entries under **H**. Gaelic words borrowed from English words starting with an **h** often drop this initial **h,** especially older words; so **ad** 'hat', **adag** 'haddock', and so on. More modern words however – and there are an increasing number of these – such as **hipidh** 'hippy' and **heileacoptar** 'helicopter', keep the **h**.

Yet **h** is one of the most common letters on any page of Gaelic, and as a result has become the victim of its own popularity. In pseudo- or pidgin Gaelic it is widely used by many who do not know the language well and feel that the liberal insertion of a few examples of **h** will give a more authentic flavour to their Gaelic. The 'greengrocer's apostrophe' plays a similar role in English, to the extent that many foreigners (and natives) think that it's an obligatory feature of English plurals. Consequently there are many shops in Paris advertising *jean's* for sale.

An example of a common misuse of **h** in Gaelic is found in the phrase *skean* (or *skene*) *dhu*, a black knife, usually worn ceremonially inside the top of a sock. This is not Gaelic spelling, the correct form being **sgian-dubh**. *Sk* is used in the phonetic form since **sg** is not an English letter group, but *–ean* and *–ene* suggest that the word is a monosyllable; since **sgian** is in fact two syllables, *skeeən* would be better phonetics. The **bh** in **dubh** is not sounded (see under **B**), so **dubh** is often written in pseudo-Gaelic as *dhu*, with an **h** added. This form was much used by Scottish literary figures such as Sir Walter Scott (eg 'Pibroch of Donuil Dhu'). Presumably *du* looked too Germanic, so inserting an **h** would make it seem more Gaelic. Scott, of course, was no Gaelic scholar, and could probably count on a similar ignorance on the part of his readers. Unfortunately, however, the combination **dh** followed by a **u** doesn't give a **d** sound in Gaelic. Instead, it has a **gh** sound (see under **D**), a bit like English *ghost*, with stronger aspiration.

This is why **Muileann Dhàibhidh** (Davie's Mill – though there are other interpretations) has the form Milngavie in English (**bh** again not sounded). Ironically, since **sgian** is a feminine noun, **sgian-dhubh** would not be wrong, but it is rarely found because of the effect of the final **n** (see under **N**).

Still, Scott was slightly nearer the mark with Donuil. **Dòmhnall** normally appears in English as Donald, and Scottish English often adds a **d** at the end of names and place-names ending in **l** or **n**. Hence Dugal**d** (Gaelic **Dùghall**), Lamon**d** (Gaelic, from Norse **Laomann**), Clelan**d** (Gaelic **MacIllfhaolain**), Lomon**d** (Gaelic **Laomainn**), Almon**d** (Gaelic **Aman**), Drummon**d** (Gaelic **Druiminn**) and so on.[1]

Although **h** is frequently found in pseudo-Gaelic, it is also very common in authentic Gaelic. This is because its main purpose, as mentioned above, is to follow immediately

---

1. This feature also appears in names of non-Gaelic origin, as Hen**d**ry (Henry), Salmon**d** (Solomon).

another consonant **when the occasion demands it**, and the point of the **h** is to indicate that the consonant immediately in front of it has changed its sound. As this suggests, most consonants in Gaelic have two sounds, the simple one and the one represented by having an **h** after it. As each consonant is discussed throughout this book their different sounds will be illustrated in turn – although not all consonants use **h** in this way.

This change is called lenition, which means softening (it used to be called aspiration), and is fundamental to Gaelic. The softening refers to the fact that the consonant is less strongly articulated. So **dh** is a lenited (aspirated) consonant.

This use of the letter **h** has not always been the only Gaelic way of showing lenition. In earlier centuries a dot above the letter did the same thing, ie indicated that the consonant had made its sound shift. Irish did this until quite recently and older signposts etc. in Ireland still have the dot. In this country there is a good example to be seen in the Glasgow Transport Museum on a fire engine of around the 1920s from Galway Urban Council. The word Council (**comhairle** in both Scottish and Irish Gaelic) is written **comhairle** and the lenited letters in the rest of the fire engine's trademark also have a dot above them.

The instance of **dh** with a **u** mentioned above raises a further point. As indicated, this **dh** has a **gh** sound, so why not just write **gh**? In fact Gaelic sometimes used to be written phonetically in this way – in some 16th and 17th century poetry, for example – and Manx Gaelic (Isle of Man), which is quite close to Scottish Gaelic, is mostly written in English phonetic script. So too is Welsh, to a degree.

But writing Gaelic phonetically (ie in <u>English</u> phonetics) has disadvantages, as any etymological connection is harder to see. Because Gaelic is an Indo-European language (of the Celtic family) it has similarities with other European languages such as English (of the Germanic family). Many Gaelic words are cognate with English words – **màthair** and *mother*, for instance.

In the case of **dh** mentioned above an example would be **ruadh**, 'brownish-red'. A phonetic Gaelic spelling would be *ruagh*, but the disappearance of the **d** makes it harder to see the link with the English cognate 'ruddy' (or the Welsh *rhudd*). Since seeing links like this can make it easier to remember the meaning of Gaelic words, correct spelling is an advantage.

Also, the same word may look rather different. Still with **dh**, take the word **gàrradh** 'garden'. Its plural is **gàrraidhean** (where the **dh** has a **y** sound, not **gh** as before – see under **D**). Manx Gaelic, which as mentioned above is written phonetically, has *garey*, 'garden' and *garaghyn*, 'gardens'. To those who do not know Manx it is not immediately obvious that these are the same word; and the change from Gaelic **dh** to Manx **gh** disguises the connection with the English cognate *garden*.

Since a word can exist in Gaelic without an **h** in it (unlenited) or with an **h** (lenited), it is important to know whether an **h** should be inserted, and why and when. What we are concerned with here is the beginning of a word. Words can, of course, have lenited consonants elsewhere in them – in the middle or end, as **Dàibhidh**, **gàrradh** and others mentioned above. But such lenited consonants do not change; they have been lenited in Gaelic for centuries for reasons of pronunciation, and the process cannot be reversed, ie the spelling *gàrrad* is not allowed. There are very occasional exceptions to this, such as **àraid** and **àraidh**, 'special, particular', both forms being in current use, or **laimrig** and **laimhrig** 'jetty', the former being the more common.

So as a rule it is only the first consonant of a word which has the option of having an **h** after it, and not all consonants do it. Whether an **h** is required or not is a matter of grammar, and any grammar book will explain the rules.

Very briefly the most important are:

1. to make the past tense, so **tog** 'lift', **thog** 'lifted';

2. an adjective after a feminine noun, as **Màiri dhubh** 'dark-haired Mairi';

3. a feminine noun after the definite article (and both masculine and feminine nouns in other cases), so **a' bheinn** 'the mountain, ben';

4. after a few words like **mo** 'my', **do** 'your', **a** 'his', **ath** 'next', **glè** 'very'; hence the popular house name **Mo Dhachaigh** 'my home'.

This feature of initial lenition is one of the things which makes spoken Gaelic difficult at first for adult learners, since the sound of the beginning of the word may change considerably, as in **tog/thog** mentioned above where **thog** loses the **t** sound – see under **T**. In many other languages, such as the Romance languages (French etc.), changes occur at the end of a word, not at the beginning, so a listener has a better chance of recognising the word, even if he/she doesn't always grasp the subtleties of the endings. But there can be compensations. The vowel in the past tense (or any other tense) of Gaelic regular verbs doesn't change. So there is nothing like English 'fling' (present)/'flung' (past), this being quite a common feature of English verbs. To a monoglot Gaelic speaker of old these might well have seemed to be two different verbs. After all, to give a Gaelic instance with the same vowels, **thig** and **thug** are two quite different verbs, meaning 'come' and 'gave' respectively.

Lenition is a very common feature of the Celtic languages, but it is not confined to them. The Tuscan dialect of Italian has *la forta* for the standard *la porta* (the door), for instance; and the disappearance of consonants inside a French word when it is flanked by vowels is very similar to Gaelic internal lenition. As will be seen later under letters **B D G M** and **T**, these consonants followed by an **h** often lose their sound inside or at the end of a Gaelic word (so **taigh** 'house'; English words like 'si**gh**t', 'hi**gh**' and 'throu**gh**out' do the same). Even if the letter does not take an **h** after it, as in the case of **l** (see under **L**), its sound can still be lost; the surname Tough is from **tulach** 'a hill'. French, of course, just drops such letters from both sound <u>and</u> spelling, as *boire* 'to drink' (Latin bi**b**ere), *croire* 'to believe' (Latin cre**d**ere), *lire* 'to read' (Latin le**g**ere), *père* 'father' (Latin pa**t**er), *dire* 'to say' (Latin di**c**ere).[2] The process is widespread. **Ch** (as in lo**ch**), often regarded as a quintessential Gaelic sound, can disappear in Manx Gaelic, as Manx *feed*, Gaelic **fichead** 'twenty'. This is very much a feature of Manx, even more than Gaelic, where a consonant in the middle of a word is softened so much that it disappears.

One is reminded of the Scots glottal stop – as in the often quoted case of a character giving his name as 'Patterson, wi twa tees', and pronouncing neither.

---

2. This very important feature of Gaelic can also be seen in English. *Frail* and *fragile* are both the same word, but the former has been borrowed from French *frêle* (from Latin *fragilis*), where the lenited **g** has disappeared, whereas the latter was a later literary borrowing straight from Latin, so the **g** remains. Similarly with *rule/regulate*, *sure/se**c**ure* etc.

So why is the letter **h** used in this way in Gaelic? If you are going to use a letter, and not the superimposed dot mentioned earlier, then **h** is the only feasible candidate, since the other letters all have sounds of their own. **H** is really just a breathing, and is rarely found on its own; and lenited consonants have some air coming through – in other words, making a lenited sound doesn't involve a closure of some sort in the mouth as with most of the unlenited consonants. So **h** is an appropriate letter to indicate this.

The adoption of the Roman alphabet to replace Ogham in the 6th century by Irish scribes was also a factor. By this time Latin was using the combinations *ch*, *ph* and *th*, the first two with sounds similar to Irish lenited **c** and **p** (and **th** in early/middle Irish had a sound similar to English *th*), so this would suggest a good reason to use **h** with other consonants. And, just as in Gaelic, other languages use **h** to indicate that a consonant has changed its sound; *ch*, *ph*, *sh*, *th* and *wh* have different sounds in English from the same letters without the **h**, and Italian and Portuguese use **h** for the same purpose. So Gaelic is in good company.

B

Beith(e) – the birch tree
This is also the modern Gaelic word.

B has both a voiced and a voiceless/unvoiced sound in Gaelic. This is a feature of other Gaelic consonants and is something to be aware of if you want to pronounce a word properly. The voiced sound is a deeper, more resonant sound of a consonant. Gaelic shares this feature with English and other languages, and the letters in question are: voiced/voiceless, b/p; d/t; g/k(c); v/f; z/s.

The first three are a feature of the Welsh soft mutations; the change from **p** to **b** for instance in that language is well illustrated by the surnames Parry and Barry, which are the same name (son of Harry).

The difference between Gaelic and English is that usually, but not always, the latter clearly distinguishes between a voiced or voiceless consonant by using the appropriate letter. Gaelic frequently doesn't. So, for instance, it is clear how the English words *sob* and *stop* sound, their final consonants being different. But Gaelic **stob** 'thrust' and **sop** 'wisp' have the same final consonant sound because the **b** of **stob** is voiceless.

It's like the English (but the other way round) use of **s**, which is usually voiceless (*so*), but voiced (=z) at the end of a word (*is*). **Th** is another English example, sometimes being

19

voiceless (*thin*), and sometimes voiced (*this*). Native speakers always get the right one, but learners often don't, which partly accounts for their accented English. So if you want to pronounce a Gaelic word like a native speaker you should bear all this in mind.

At the beginning of a word **b** is pronounced like an English **b**, as **baile** (*balə*) 'town'. Elsewhere, as noted above, it is, in the vast majority of cases, like English **p**, as **obair** (**o** as in *so*) 'work', **tobar** (**o** as in *so*) 'a well' etc. This is why **Ceann Loch Gilb** is Lochgilphead in English, and the name **Gilleasbaig** is Gillespie, and so on. In such instances it isn't written with a **p** in Gaelic because that often wouldn't give quite the right sound – see under **P**.

This unvoiced sound of **b** is also a feature of German, where **b** at the end of a word has a **p** sound, and this is also what lies behind English *scribe/ script, nubile/ nuptial* etc.

In some areas **b** seems to be not sounded at all when preceded by an **m**, as in **tìr nam beann** (*tcheer nəm yown*) 'land of the mountains'. This is called nasalisation (or eclipsis), also a feature of Irish, Manx and Welsh, the last two of which remove it from the spelling; 'in Bangor' is *ym Mangor* in Welsh.

B can also be lenited, ie be written **bh**, and its sound is like English **v**, as **bha** (*va*) 'was', 'were'. In other Celtic languages, as Manx, it is actually written **v** (and **f** in the case of Welsh, where a single **f** has a **v** sound, as in English *of*). Elsewhere, a Russian **b** has a **v** sound; so does **b** in modern Greek (though not in Classical Greek), which means, as visitors to the country will have noticed, that common international words like 'bar' (pub) and 'beer' can't start with a **b** in Greek script (it uses the letters **mp** instead). Spanish sounds **v** and **b** the same (both like **b**), and the same interchange is found in the Germanic language group, eg English *have* and German *haben*. So there is nothing unusual about Gaelic's treatment of a lenited **b**.

As mentioned above, **bh**, in common with other lenited consonants, is often not sounded in the middle or at the end of a word. Whether a **bh** is sounded or not sometimes depends on the district and/or the speaker, so you will hear **àbhaist** (*aa(v)istch*) 'usual' with, or without, the **v** sound; and in place-names it is sounded in **Port na h-Abhainne**, Portnahaven, 'Port of the River' in Islay, but not in **Geàrraidh na h-Aibhne,** Garynahine, 'piece of land by the river' in Lewis. The different spellings of the genitive of **abhainn** seem to reflect this.

In English versions of Gaelic placenames, **v** is sometimes written but not pronounced, as in Milngavie (**Muileann Dhàibhidh**); and sometimes it's not written, as in Rhu (**an Rubha** – the promontory). So things can be quite confusing.

Not sounding a **v** on occasions is something many people should be familiar with, since it's a feature of Scots as found in *hae*, *gie*, *hairst*, and so on, as well as English pairings such as provident/ prudent, movement/ momentum.

Bh at the end of a word often has a weak **oo** sound (as in English *foot*) in some dialects. So **agaibh** 'at you' sometimes sounds like *akoo*, **leanabh** 'child' like *lyenoo*. (Manx spells it *lhiannoo*). This is why **A' Bheinn Mheanbh** 'the small mountain' has the English form Ben Venue; and why **sliabh** 'a hill(side)' appears as Slew (eg Slewfad ie **Sliabh Fada**) in many locations in the Rinns of Galloway. Manx, tellingly, has *slieau*.

C

Coll – the hazel tree
The modern word is **Calltainn**.

C is always a hard sound in Gaelic, like English **k**, so it never has the soft sound found in English (*cent*, *cite* – same sound as *sent*, *site*; this English use of **c** could be seen as another instance of an unnecessary use of a letter for etymological reasons).

C can be regarded as the defining consonant of the Gadelic (Gaelic, Irish, Manx) family as opposed to the Brythonic (Welsh, Breton), since an Indo-European **qu** became **k** (now written **c**) in Gaelic, but **p** in Welsh. So Gaelic **mac** 'son' was Welsh *map*, later *ap*, hence names like Pritchard (son of Richard) etc. Manx Gaelic does the same, hence Quilliam, Kissock (son of William, Isaac) etc. English, with its Classical background, also has this **p** and **q** interchange, as *pentagon* and *quintet*, both based on the meaning 'five'. One curious effect of this was that St. **P**atrick, the patron saint of Ireland, wasn't called this when he lived in Ireland due to the absence of **p** from the alphabet (see also under **P**) but was known as **C**odrige or similar. In modern Gaelic, however, Patrick is **Pàdraig**.

A single **c** is frequently sounded *chk*, as in Lo*ch* *K*atrine, in the middle and at the end of a word. So **mac**, mentioned above, sounds like *machk* (**ch** as in lo**ch**). This sound is also written in full, as it were, in the form **chd** in many words, so that **bochd** 'poor', **beannachd** 'blessing' are pronounced *bochk* and *byannæchk* (both with **ch** as in lo**ch**). What has happened here is that such words originally had a double c; the first one was then lenited, the second remained as it was, and the end result is the *chk* sound, written today **chd**.

In modern Gaelic a double **c** is not found; the only consonants which can be doubled are **l**, **n** and **r**.

A lenited **c**, ie **ch**, is like the sound of **ch** in **loch** when it is next to a broad vowel, but has a lighter sound when in contact with a slender vowel; so **chi** 'will see' sounds more like *hee*. Throughout this book, however, for reasons of simplicity I have used the phrase **ch** as in lo**ch** to indicate that the sound is **not** an English *ch* (as in *church*); the Gaelic sound will depend on whether the **ch** is next to a broad or a slender vowel. This is one consonant in Gaelic which doesn't lose its sound completely in the middle of a Gaelic word as other lenited consonants do, though it is, of course, softened from a hard **c**. As mentioned earlier (under **H**), the **c** can disappear internally from French and Manx, and Scots has this feature too, as *taen* (English *taken*).

For **cn** sounded as **cr** see under **N**.

D

Dair – Oak
The modern form is **Darach**.

A simple **d** has three sounds in Gaelic, depending on whether it is next to a broad or a slender/narrow vowel, or at the end of a word. This distinction between the type of vowel is crucial to Gaelic spelling and pronunciation, so it is important to be aware of the difference. Fortunately, English observes the same distinction on occasions. The broad vowels are **a,o** and **u,** and the slender ones are **e** and **i**. In English their use affects the sound of the letter **c**, as *cat, cot, cut*, but *cell* and *city* – a harder sound with the broad vowels and a softer one with the slender vowels. So it is with many Gaelic consonants.

D with a broad vowel is close to the hard **d** sound of English *dog*, so **dona** 'bad', **dàil** (*daal*) 'delay'. With a slender vowel it has a softer sound, like the beginning of the English word *deuce*, or the Scottish surnames Dewar, Durie etc.; in other words, a **j** or **dy** sound. (An apparent exception to this rule in a Gaelic word, for instance **ged** 'though' – pronounced with the **d** hard – is very rare and may be accounted for by the fact that the vowel in this word often has an **a** sound.) The Gaelic alphabet doesn't have the letters **j** or **y**, so instead it uses **d** with slender vowels to make this sound. English, of course, can also use a **g** to make this sound, as *gem*, so when borrowing words from English, Gaelic will use **d** with a slender vowel to represent both the **j** and the soft **g** sounds. So **dinichean** is *jeans* and **deilignit** is *gelignite*. This is why the island of Jura is **Diùra**, and **Am Bàrr Dearg** (a few miles north of Dumfries) is Barjarg.

When Gaelic borrows words from English or other languages starting with a **d**, such as *diesel* (Gaelic **dìosail**) etc, it generally sounds them as in English, with a hard **d** – in other words, they are exceptions to the **d** with the slender vowel rule mentioned above.

The third sound of **d** mentioned above occurs when it is inside a word or ends a word after a short vowel. In this case it is unvoiced, ie sounded like a **t**, so **rud** 'a thing' sounds rather like English *root*, and **dad** 'anything' sounds like *dat*. This is also a feature of German, which led Sir Walter Scott to write vel**t**-mareschal for fel**d**-marschall (field marshal), in 'A Legend of Montrose'. And in Welsh **d** is a soft mutation of **t**, while the Scottish surname Bee**d**ie is a variant of Bea**tt**ie. English forms such as **t**wo/**d**uo, quatrain/quadrangle also illustrate the point.

As indicated under **C**, **d** after **ch** has a **k** sound, as **bàrdachd** 'poetry', (baardachk – **ch** as in lo**ch**).

D can also be lenited, and the resulting **dh** has two different sounds depending on the vowel it is with. When it is with a broad vowel (**a,o,u**) it has a **gh** sound, a bit like English *ghost* but with a bit more breathing/aspiration, as mentioned above. So **glè dhoirbh** (*glay ghərəv*) 'very hard', **achadh** (*achəgh* – **ch** as in lo**ch**) 'a field', and hence Milngavie, **Muileann Dh**àibhidh mentioned earlier, and **Cama-Dh**ail (by Fort William) which is Cama**gh**ael, 'crooked field' in English. When **dh** is with a slender vowel (**e, i**) it has a **y** sound like English *yes*. So **dhiùlt** (*yoolt*) 'refused'. It should be noted, however, that there is an increasing tendency to pronounce **dh** with a broad vowel as if it were with a slender vowel. So one often hears **dh'aithnich** 'recognised', **a dh'fhaicinn** 'to see' (**fh** not sounded – see under **F**) with a **y** sound at the beginning.

However, **dh** is often not sounded inside or at the end of a word, and this is particularly the case when it is with a slender vowel. In **chaidh** (*chai* – **ch** as in lo**ch**) 'went' and **ag ràdh** (*ə krah* – stress on the *a*) 'saying', for instance, the **dh** has no sound. Hence place names such as **Earra-Ghàidheal** (Argyll), **Am Baile Nodha** (Balinoe 'the new settlement' – Tiree, Black Isle) are written without the **dh** in their English transliterations. Indeed, because of the fact that **dh** is so often silent internally with slender vowels, it is inserted artificially into words borrowed from English, as **cidhe** 'quay', **paidhir** 'a pair' etc. to separate the syllables. This is artificial in that **d** does not belong to these words from an etymological viewpoint, but is presumably inserted by analogy with words like **cridhe** 'heart'. In this word the **dh** is, as so often, silent, but properly belongs to the word, as the English cognate *cardiac* shows. Other consonants which are used artificially in this way are **g** and **t** (see under these letters).

After the letters **l** and **n**, **d** is not always lenited where it might be expected to be. Gaelic songs feature **mo nighean donn** (*mo neeən down*) 'my brown-haired maid', where **d** remains unlenited even though it follows the feminine noun **nighean**; likewise **aon duine** 'one man' but **aon bhalach** 'one boy'. Similarly with **l** we sometimes have **sgoil dubh** 'the black arts, witchcraft', although **sgoil** 'school' is feminine.

The treatment of **d** after **an** in Lewis Gaelic is also notable. Here the sound of **d** often disappears, so that **an-diugh** 'today', sounds like *ən yoo*. This is called nasalisation and happens in Lewis with the letter **t** also (see under **T**). As noted earlier it is also a feature of Welsh, so 'in Dolgellau' is sounded and written *yn Nolgellau*.

The recent replacement of **d** by **t** after **s** should also be noted. It is now recommended that words such as **furasda** 'easy' be written **furasta**, **èisd** 'listen' be written **èist**, and so on. Many Gaelic books will of course have the old form and standard dictionaries may not contain the new spelling; **furasta**, for instance, doesn't appear in Dwelly's classic Gaelic-English dictionary.

F

Feàrn – alder
The modern form is **Feàrna**.

This letter is sounded as it is in English, ie unvoiced (unlike Welsh, where it is voiced, so sounds like **v**). Gaelic **f** is from the Indo-European **v**, however, as various cognates show, eg **fear** (*fer*) 'man', Latin *vir*, English *virile*. It is found at the beginning of Gaelic words, but may occasionally be seen inside a word, as **difir** 'differ', **deifir**, 'haste'.

Lenited **f, ie fh,** is normally silent, and is usually followed immediately by a vowel, or occasionally by **l** or **r**; so **nas fheàrr** 'better' is pronounced *nass yaar*. So **Cill Fhinn** 'white church' in Perthshire is Killin, and **A' Bheinn Fhada** 'the long mountain' in Kintail is Ben Attow, reflecting the fact that the Gaelic **fh** has no sound.

This lenition means that a word starting with **f** will frequently be found without the **f** sound, which has sometimes led to the situation where the basic word is regarded as starting with a vowel. Confusion still exists, so that today **eagal** (*ekəl*) and **feagal** 'fear' are both found, as are **àileadh** (*aaləgh*) and **fàileadh** 'a smell'. The **f** does not belong to such words, as can be seen from another instance, **fàinne** 'a ring', English cognates of which are *anus*, *annular*, or from Welsh equivalents: Gaelic **fuar** 'cold' is Welsh *oer*, and **fagasachd** 'nearness, proximity' is Welsh <u>*agosrwydd*</u>. This uncertainty is rather like the treatment of an initial **h** in the colloquial speech of southern England, where it can be added and removed indiscriminately. So one hears *the 'andlebars* and, conversely, *the hashtray*.

There is a curious echo of this Gaelic treatment of lenited **f** to be found in Spanish. Spanish is, of course, a Latin language, but words which start with **f** in Latin lose the **f** in Spanish (except words beginning **fr-** and **fu-**), putting a now silent **h** in its place. So *hablar* 'to talk', Latin *fabulare*, English *fable*. A Celtic language was spoken in Spain long before (and presumably for some time after) the Roman conquest, which may account for this interesting feature. Or there may be the influence of another Iberian language to consider: Basque, still spoken in the north west of Spain, has no **f** sound.

There are just three exceptions to silent **fh** in Gaelic, all of them common, where **fh** has an **h** sound: **fhathast** (*ha-əst*) 'yet, still'; **fhèin** (*hane*) 'self'; and **fhuair** (*hooer*) 'got, found'. The last, however, has the normal **fh** sound – ie no sound – in the negative and in subordinate clauses; so **cha d'fhuair** (*cha dooer*) 'did not get'.

G

Gort – Ivy
The modern word is **Eidheann**.

G in Gaelic is always hard, like the **g** in English *get*, not soft like the **g** in *gem*. So **garbh** (*garav*) 'rough'. When it occurs at the end of a word it is unvoiced (sounded like a **k**); so **tig** 'come' sounds like *tcheek*, **bog** 'damp' like *boke*. German does this too, and **g** is a soft mutation of **c** in Welsh. So we find **Carraig** 'rock' as Carri**ck** in English, and **Cill Mheàrnaig** as Kilmarno**ck**.

When **g** is lenited it has the same sound as **dh**, ie a **gh** (*gh*ost, with stronger aspiration) sound with **a, o** and **u,** and a **y** (*yes*) sound with **e** and **i**. This **y** sound provides a timely reminder of the correct pronunciation of the place name Dalziel (**Dail Gheal** 'white field' – Inverness etc.), where the **z** is not an English **z** but rather the old Scots letter yogh which had a **y** sound, as indicated by the modern spelling of the surname Dalyell.

As mentioned with **dh, gh** is frequently not sounded inside or at the end of a word (like English si**gh**t, si**gh** etc), and **gh** was sometimes written for **dh** and vice versa, especially when they were silent. **Troidh**, for instance, was an earlier form of **troigh** 'a foot', but the latter is now the accepted spelling. So **gh** is silent in **faigh** (*fie*) 'get', **foghlam** (*fǝlǝm*) 'education'. This is why **Ceann Tràgha** (Argyll) 'head of the beach' is Kintra or Kentra in English. So, as with other lenited consonants, **gh** is sometimes inserted into a word between vowels even though it has no etymological connection with the word. Thus we find **ogha** (*oa* – **o** as in English *go*) 'grandchild'. The combination *oa*, it should be noted, is not found in Gaelic, just as *ao* is not an English vowel group (*gaol* notwithstanding). So inserting an unconnected **gh** between the vowels gets round this problem. This is also why the Oa promontory in Islay has to have a slightly different form in Gaelic; it appears as **An Obha**, and again the **bh** has no original connection with the word. The same could be said of **motha** 'greater', where the *oa* is separated by yet another different silent lenited consonant which also has no connection with the word. An alternative form in use, **mò**, simplifies matters somewhat.

This change of a lenited **g** into a *y* sound has parallels elsewhere. In English itself we have pairs of the same origin such as royal/regal, loyal/legal, yard/garden etc. Scots has *yett* for English *gate*, hence the place name Yetts o Muckart. German often has a **g** where English has a **y** (with both broad and slender vowels), as *Weg/way*; *gelb/yellow*; *garn/yarn* etc. And in modern Greek a **g** (gamma) has a *y* sound with several Greek vowels; hence the many places (a bit like the numerous examples of Llan- in Wales, of similar meaning) beginning *ayia* or *ayios* (sacred, saint), as Ayia Napa in Cyprus. (A gamma is now officially transliterated by a *g* in Roman script but the sound remains *y*.)

This change is still happening in the Gaelic of today, where a **gh** <u>sound</u> (ie **gh** with broad vowels) is moving to a **y** sound (see under **D**).

For **gn** sounded as **gr** see under **N**.

L

Luis – the quicken tree, a form of rowan
The modern word for rowan is **Caorann**.

A single **l** has two sounds in Gaelic. One is the so-called dark **l**, or back **l**, a sound which doesn't really exist in English, but the **l** in *although* is a bit like it. It's a very distinctive Gaelic sound, and is found when **l** is next to a broad vowel. So **latha** (*la-ə*) 'day' (sometimes written **là**), **loch** 'lake, loch'. This means that there is a difference, albeit slight, between the pronunciation of **loch** in Gaelic and in English; so the **l** of **Inbhir Lòchaidh** (near Fort William) sounds different in Gaelic from that in the English *Inverlochy* – as does the **o**, which is usually short in the English pronunciation of this word but long in Gaelic, as the accent over the **ò** shows. But this is not surprising, since the word has been anglicised. Gaelic treats words borrowed from English in its own way too; **lagh** 'law' has the dark **l**, but English *law*, of course, doesn't. An instance with a different letter is **acaire** 'acre', where the Gaelic form has a *chk* sound as explained under **C**.

Unlenited **l** with slender vowels (**e** and **i**) is like an English **l** with a *y* sound (as in *yes*) immediately following, like the **ll** sound in *million*; so **leathann** (*ly-ehən*) 'broad', **lìon** (*lyeeən*) 'a net'. This applies only at the beginning of the word; inside or at the end a double **l** is used, as **buille** 'a blow', **tuill** 'holes'.

But in the middle of a word **ll** with a slender vowel sometimes has just an ordinary **l** sound, not a *ly* sound. So **seillean** 'a bee' is pronounced *shellən*, and **saillte** 'salted' is *sigh-ltchə.* This is also the case in certain areas at the end of a word, as **till** (*tcheel*) 'return', **fèill** (*fayl*) 'festival'.

L is one of the letters in the Gaelic alphabet which doesn't have an **h** after it in writing (the others being **n** and **r**). But it is still lenited in sound if necessary. The lenited broad **l** is not much different from the unlenited, but the lenited slender **l** is quite noticeable, the *y* sound disappearing. So **leum** (*lame*) 'leapt' is the past tense of **leum** (*lyame*) 'leap', the past tense being lenited as explained under **H**. This lenited form is also found with the common word **le** 'with', and is the normal sound when found internally or at the end of a word; so **eile** (*ailə*) 'other', **caileag** (*kalak*) 'girl', **mil** (*meel*) 'honey', **sil** (*sheel*) 'to shed'.

As mentioned above, **l**, like **n** and **r**, can also be doubled. When **ll** comes after **a** or **o** at the end of a word <u>of one syllable</u> the vowel sound is altered (but not in Islay). This is a feature of English too; double consonants are not pronounced double (unless they are part of a compound word, as *disservice* etc.). So there is no difference in the **p** sound in the middle of *leper* and *pepper*. But like Gaelic **ll**, English double consonants frequently indicate a change of vowel sound from words with the single consonant: *bated/batted*; *filed/filled*; *holy/holly* etc. So in Gaelic **call** 'loss' is pronounced rather like English *cowl*, whereas **càl** 'kale', with a single **l**, is pronounced *kaal* (vowel sound rather like *shall*). Similarly **gal** 'weep', but **gall** (*gowl*, as in *scowl*) 'stranger', and **poll** (*powl*) 'a pit'. This will also happen if there is an **e** before the **a**, as **geall** (*gyowl*) 'bet', but not an **i**, since **ciall** (*keeal*) 'sense' has the stress on the **i** and not on the **-all** as in the previous instances – see under **ia**. In other words, **ciall** is a word of two syllables, and the same happens with words like **barrall** 'shoe lace' where the stress is on **barr-**, and so **–all** doesn't have the *–owl* sound; the word is pronounced *barəl*. If the **–all** part of a word moves forward from being the last syllable, then it also usually loses its -*owl* sound; so **dall** (*dowl*) 'blind', but **dalladh** (*daləgh*) 'blinding', **ball** (*bowel* – but just one syllable) 'member', **balla** (*balə*) 'wall'.

This may explain the place name Toward at the south of the Cowal peninsula. It is pronounced *Tow* (as in English *now*) *Ard*, is stressed on the first syllable, and was originally spelled Tollard, (the modern Gaelic spelling) 'deep hole' being one possible meaning.[1] As we have just seen, this would give the vowel sound of the pronunciation of Toward when it was two separate words. Interestingly, the similarly named English village of Tollard Royal (though of Celtic origin, meaning 'hollowed-out hill') doesn't – not surprisingly – show any sign of the vowel change effected by Gaelic.

Gaelic also has this vowel change with words borrowed from English, as **ball** 'a ball', again pronounced a bit like *bowel* but just one syllable); so **ball-coise** (*bowel coshə*) 'football'.

A final **l** also usually – but not in some districts – prevents a word starting with **d** or **t** from being lenited where it might be expected – see under **D** and **T**.

Another feature of **l** in Gaelic words is found in **Alba** (*Alapə*) 'Scotland'. As can be seen there is an unstressed vowel sound between the **l** and the **b**. Scots should be familiar with this feature as it is commonly found in Scottish English; so film is pronounced *filəm*, girl is pronounced *girəl*, and so on. In Gaelic this unstressed vowel, or occasionally schwa, can occur when **l** is followed by **b**, **bh**, **ch**, **g**, **m**, **mh** and **p**, as in the following words: **Alba, Loch Gilb**, mentioned earlier (*Giləp*); **falbh** (*falav*) 'go away, leave'; **tulchann** (*tooləchan*) 'gable'; **sealg** (*shalak*)

---

1. This change from **ll** to **w** is a feature of Scots. The fish pollan is called powan in Scotland.

'hunt'; **salm** (*salam*) 'psalm'; **talmhainn** (*talavin*) 'of (the) earth'; **calpa** (*kalapa*) 'calf' (of the leg). There are occasional exceptions to this, as **Sgalpaigh** 'Scalpay' (Harris), and, borrowed from English, **ceilp** 'kelp', neither of which have this extra schwa sound.

M

Muin – the Vine
Modern words are **Fìonan** and **Crann-fìona**.

M has the sound of an English **m**, so **mac** (*machk* – **ch** as in lo**ch**) 'son'. When it occurs after **o** and **a** at the end of a monosyllable it often affects the sound of the **o** (but not in Islay), so **trom** 'heavy' sounds like *trowm* (vowel sound as in *brown*), **lom** 'bare' like *lowm*, and so on. An instance with **a** is **àm** 'time', which sounds like *owm* and the same sound appears in modern borrowings from English, as **dam** 'a dam'.

This is like the use of final **ll** and **nn**, mentioned under these letters, with the difference that only a single **m** is used (double **m** is not found in Gaelic). But the words cited, and others such as **tom** (*towm*) 'hillock' and **crom** (*crowm*) 'bent, crooked' were written with a double **m** in earlier stages of Irish. If it's not a monosyllable, this means that the stress will be on the first syllable, which, as noted before, is the rule in Gaelic, and not on the last. So in the word **aotrom** 'not heavy, light', **trom** no longer has a stress and the sound is no longer *trowm* but simply *trom*. For a similar effect with the vowel **u** in Lewis see under U.

A lenited **m** (**mh**) is pronounced like a **v**, so **làmh** (*laav*) 'hand', **mhothaich** (*vawich* – **ch** as in lo**ch**) 'noticed'. So **An Sgeir Mhòr** 'the big sea rock' – off Mull – is Skerryvore in English, and **Port a' Mhadaidh** (Port of the dog, wolf) – in Cowal – is Portavadie. **B**, of course, also has a **v** sound when lenited, but **m** whether lenited or not gives a nasal quality to adjacent vowel(s). So **bhaoth** 'simple, silly', and **mhaoth** 'soft, tender' are not quite identical in sound; the latter has a nasal character.

Often, however, when **mh** occurs inside a word it is not pronounced; so **comhairle** 'council, counsel' sounds like *cawerl-ya*. That is why a placename such as **An Caolas Cumhang** 'the narrow strait' – in Sutherland – has the English form Kylesku, and places as far apart as Garrygannichy (South Uist) and Gannochy (Edzell, Angus/Kincardine border) both contain the word **gainmheach** 'sand' with no **v** sound.

The **v** sound is usually retained in Islay, however, especially when the **mh** is followed immediately by a consonant. So **samhradh** mentioned later in this paragraph sounds something like *sevaragh* in Islay. And just as a final **m** can give an *ow* sound to a preceding **o**, as indicated above, so a lenited **m** can create a similar sound in the middle of a word, where the **mh** is again silent. **Samhradh** 'summer', for instance, is pronounced *sowragh*, and **geamhradh** 'winter' is pronounced *gyowragh*. (Manx has *saurey* and *gaurey* respectively.) So **Drochaid Ghamhair** 'Bridge over the River Gaur' – in Perthshire – is Bridge of Gaur in English, and **Meallan a' Ghamhna** 'Hill of the Stirk' – in Ross & Cromarty – is Mellongaun.

There is a strong tendency in Uist and elsewhere to sound a final unstressed –**amh** as an *oo* sound (as in English *too*), so that **dèanamh** 'doing' is pronounced as *je-anoo* or *jee-anoo*. In Manx Gaelic this word is written *jannoo*, so this is the correct sound there. In Scottish Gaelic the pronunciation *jee-anav* would be regarded as the correct pronunciation, but in some dialects the final **v** is frequently dropped. **Bh** is often similarly treated – see under **B**. So **Àrd Thalamh** 'High Ground' – Dunoon area – appears in English as Ardhallow, and **Baile Cheathraimh** 'Quarter Land' – in Perthshire – as Pitkerro.

For **mn** sounded as **mr** see under **N**.

M is another letter which can have a schwa, or another unstressed vowel sound, after it. So **aimsir** 'weather' sounds like *emeshir*, and **timcheall** 'about' like *tchiməchyal* (second **ch** as in lo*ch*).

N

Nuin, the ash tree
The modern word is **Uinnseann**.

An unlenited single **n** when it is next to a broad vowel has a sound like English **n**. So **bun** (*boon*) 'base, foot'. When it is with a slender vowel it has a *ny* sound like the **n** in English *new*. So **nead** (*nyet*) 'a nest'. This slender **n** sound is also found inside a word, as **duine** (*doonyə*) 'man, person', but not always, as the common word **teine** (*tchenə*) 'fire' shows. A double **n** between vowels also gives this *ny* sound, as **bainne** (*banyə*) 'milk'; when it's **not** between two vowels, ie a consonant is in the way, as **cinnteach** (*keentchəch* – second **ch** as in lo**ch**) 'sure', then the *y* sound isn't heard with the **n**. And **nn** at the end of a word often has just a simple **n** sound, not a *ny* sound, as **feamainn** (*femin*) 'seaweed'.

N, like **l** and **r**, never has an **h** written after it, but it can still be lenited in sound if required. There is no real difference as far as the broad **n** is concerned, but lenited **n** with a slender vowel drops the *y* sound after it. So **nigh** (*nee*) 'washed'; the unlenited form is spelled the same but sounded *nyee*. The context of a phrase will usually tell you which sound to make, as **nigh** by itself has two possible pronunciations, depending on whether it's present tense (imperative) or past tense, just like the English verb *read*.

As mentioned above, **n**, again like **l** and **r**, can be doubled. When this happens at the end of a monosyllabic word after **a** or **ea** the **a** has an *ow* sound (as in English *now*) – but again not in Islay; so **ann** 'in', **peann** (*pyown*) 'pen', **clann** (*clown*) 'children', the last sounding quite different from English *clan* which is borrowed from it; the back **l** is different too (see under **L**). So there is a difference in the vowel sound from words ending in a single **n**, **fan** 'stay' being pronounced like English *fan*. (As mentioned under **L**, English double consonants can alter the sound of vowels too; instances with **n** would be *planed/planned*, *tiny/tinny* etc.). In similar circumstances final –**onn** sounds much the same as final –**ann**; so **tonn** 'a wave' sounds rather like English *town*. So for many Gaelic speakers **fann** 'faint, weak' and **fonn** 'a tune' have the same sound, though this would not be the case in Islay, where the two are distinguished, the **a** and the **o** having their normal sounds.

Again, as with **ll** after a broad vowel (see under **L**), the *ow(n)* sound generally reverts to a simple **a** or **o** sound in a word of two or more syllables. So **bonn** (*bown*) 'a sole, base', but **bonnach** (*bonach* – **ch** as in lo**ch**) 'bannock', **fann** (*fown*) 'faint', but **fannachadh** (*fanəchəgh* – **ch** as in lo**ch**) 'fainting'.

Placenames such as **Sanndaig** ('Sandy Bay', in Tiree), which appears as Saundaig in English, and **Na Hann** ('Harbour', in Mull – there is a Port Haunn nearby) which appears as Haunn, illustrate this feature.

N is frequently pronounced in many areas like **r** after the letters **c**, **g**, **m** and **t**, and in such cases it is written **r** in Manx. So **cnoc** 'hill' is pronounced *croc* (Manx *cronk*), and there are **mac** names which show this feature: MacCracken, for example, is a variant of the Gaelic **MacNeachdainn** (and is actually more Gaelic in pronunciation than the Anglicised form MacNaughton). In the case of the other letters mentioned, **gnùis** 'face' is pronounced *groosh* (Manx *grooish*), **mnathan** 'wives, women' is pronounced *mrahən* (Manx *mraane*), and **tnù** 'envy' is pronounced *troo* (Manx *troo*). This is why **Caol an t-Snàimh** (Narrows of the Swimming – between Cowal and Bute) appears in English as Colintraive, the letter **s** in the Gaelic form not being sounded in this case – see under **S**. It should be stressed that there is nothing wrong with pronouncing an **n** as an **n** in such cases; it is a feature of the dialect of some speakers, even if they are in a minority. English, of course, finds such combinations of letters difficult when they occur at the beginning of a word, but instead of changing the sound of the **n** as Gaelic does, it simply doesn't pronounce the previous letter, as with *knee, know, gnaw, gnome, mnemonic, pneumatic* and so on; and of course **cnoc**, mentioned above, is so treated in its Anglicised form in the many Knock placenames, and in the surname Knox.

Also, in Gaelic an **n** isn't sounded nor written when it appears in a verb borrowed from English. In such cases Gaelic generally, though not always, uses the participle (-ing) form of the English verb but reduces it to -**ig**; so *drive* is **dràibhig** (ie driving), *spell* is **speilig** and so on. Such forms are very common in everyday speech where an existing Gaelic verb doesn't immediately come to mind, or in what might be termed non-traditional Gaelic activities. So you'll hear **patròiligeadh** 'patrolling', **trèanaigeadh** 'training' and so on. The -**ig** ending is a clear sign that the verb has been borrowed from English, even for what might be considered a traditional Gaelic pursuit, as **poidsig** 'poach'. The reason for its use may be that Gaelic, unlike English, makes the present (and imperfect) tenses <u>only</u> with the participle, ie cannot say the equivalent of 'I write', but says instead 'I am (was) writing'.

In the combination **ng**, as in **fang** 'fank, sheep-fold', **pongail** 'punctual' and so on, the **g** has a full sound of its own; in other words **ng** sounds like it does in English *single*, and not as it does in English *sing*. So Gaelic **trang** 'busy' has the full **g** sound, whereas Scots *thrang* (English *throng*) from which it is borrowed has the softer English **ng** sound. There are occasional exceptions to this in some areas, where internal **ng** is often silent in words such as **iongantach** 'surprising', sometimes reflected in spelling (**ioghantach**), **ceangail** 'tie, fasten', though the nasal effect of the **n** is retained.[1]

N is another letter which can have a schwa, or other unstressed vowel, after it. This occurs with the letters **b**, **bh**, **ch**, **m**, and **mh**. So we have **cainb** 'cannabis' sounding like *keneb*, **inbhe** 'status' like *inəvə*, **muinchill** 'sleeve' like *moonichil* (**ch** as in lo**ch**), **ainm** 'name' like *enəm*, **seanmhair** 'grandmother' like *shenaver*. Sometimes the neutral vowel was written in older Gaelic, so forms such as **caineab** for **cainb** can be found in older books, and **Banbhaidh**, near Fort William, is Banavie in English.

---

1. This happens even if the **ng** is a fundamental part of the word; **ceangail** is from Latin *cingere* 'to bind', English *cingulum*.

P

Beith Bhog – soft **b**, **beith** being 'birch'
In other words, **p** is an unvoiced **b**,
and the letter is sometimes actually written *peith*.

P is not an original Gaelic letter, which accounts for its being named with reference to **b**, which it most closely resembles. We can see that it is missing from Gaelic by comparing cognates, as **athair** 'father' but Latin *pater*, Italian *padre* and so on. This is an instance of a missing initial **p**, and there are many more examples. Sometimes it can be missing inside a word, but leaves its mark in the form of other consonants more acceptable to Gaelic at the time. So **seachd** 'seven' (se**p**tet, etc), **feasgar** 'evening' (ves**p**er) and so on.

Words with **p** in Gaelic today are therefore borrowed from other languages – a well known exception being **piuthar** (*pewər*) 'sister' – mainly English, Norse and Latin, and the **p** is sounded as an English **p**. So **pìob** (*peeəp*) 'pipe'. Since **b** is often sounded like a **p** in Gaelic (see under **B**), **p** often replaces a **b** in words borrowed from English; so **ploc** (English *block*), **pràis** (English *brass*), **putan** (English *button*), showing the traditional Gaelic fondness for unvoiced consonants.

Lenited **p** (**ph**) has an **f** sound as in English *pheasant*, *fit*, never separated as in *shepherd*. So **A' Phàirc** (*ə faark*) 'The Park' – in Lewis.

When it is not initial, **p**, like **c** and **t**, has a breathing sound, an aspiration, before it, more noticeable in some areas than others. So **sop** 'a wisp of straw' sounds like *sohp*, and **tapaidh** 'strong, brave' like *tahpee*.

R

Ruis – the Elder tree
The more common modern word is **Droman**.

R has a similar sound to an English **r**, as **ràmh** (*raav*) 'oar'. Like **l** and **n**, it is never followed by an **h** in writing, though it can, in theory, be lenited, but it can be hard to distinguish between the lenited and the unlenited form; the former is possibly more voiced and with a bit more of a breathing. So place names with the (now discouraged) spelling Rhum, and the various Rhus do not reflect Gaelic spelling; they represent an attempt at a pseudo-Gaelic effect as mentioned under **H**.

R, again like **l** and **n**, can be doubled, but this does not have an effect on the sound of the preceding vowel as it does in the case of **l** and **n** (see under **L** and **N**). A double **r** (standing for an earlier **r**+consonant) does have the advantage of helping to distinguish between words which are otherwise similar, as **cor** 'state, condition' and **còrr** 'odd, uneven', particularly since the latter is sometimes found written without an accent.

It is possible that a final –**rr** was more strongly trilled than –**r**, but this distinction is sometimes hard to hear nowadays. So words borrowed from English can have either, as **càr** 'car' but **teàrr** (*tchyaar*) 'tar'.

A feature with final –**r** after a slender vowel is found in some areas, eg much of the Western Isles, in which the **r** is sounded so lightly that it is almost like English **th** (voiced, as in *this*), so that **air** 'on' sounds a bit like *aith*.

Also very common is the so-called sibilant **r**, where the combination **rt** is sounded *rst*. So **ceart** 'right' sounds like *kyarst*, **ort** 'on you' like *orst* and so on. Indeed, it is relatively unusual to hear such words without the **s** sound, except in Islay. This also happens in some areas with **rd**, so that **òrd** 'a hammer' sounds like *awrsd*.

R is another letter which can have a schwa, or another unstressed vowel, after it, and this happens with the letters **b**, **bh**, **ch**, **g**, **gh**, and **m**. So **earbsa** 'confidence' is pronounced *erəbsə*, **garbh** 'rough' is pronounced *garav*, **dorch** 'dark' is pronounced *dawroch* (**ch** as in lo**ch**), **dearg** 'red' is pronounced *jerak*, **Borgh** 'Borve' – a common placename – is pronounced *borogh*, and **gorm** 'blue' is pronounced *gorom* (**o** as in *for* in the last two). As mentioned under **N**, this neutral vowel was sometimes written in older Gaelic: Pont's map of Kintyre in about 1590 has Bellochgor**u**m (now Belloch).

S

Sùil – Willow
The modern word is **Seileach**.

S with a broad vowel (**a,o,u**) has a sound like an English **s** in *see*, so **salach** 'dirty', **solas** 'light'. In other words, it is unvoiced and so not sounded like the **s** in *his*, which has the voiced **z** sound. This **z** is the normal sound for an internal and a final **s** after a vowel in English, the unvoiced sound being indicated by **ss**, as *hiss*; if it's after a consonant it may be voiced or unvoiced depending on the consonant – as *cats*, but *dogs* (dogz). So Gaelic **is** (*iss* or *us*) 'am, is, are' is pronounced differently from English *is*.

    S with a slender vowel (**e, i**) immediately next to it has a sound equivalent to English **sh.** So **sean** 'old' is pronounced *shen*, **sìth** 'peace' is pronounced *shee*, and **Baile a' Chaolais** on Loch Leven is *Ballachulish*, and **Siabost** in Lewis is *Shawbost*. The difference between the two sounds of **s** can sometimes be seen in the same word, as **sìos** 'down', pronounced *sheeass*; or notice the difference between **fios** 'knowledge' (*feess*) and **fois** 'rest, peace' (*fosh*). An exception to this is the above-mentioned **is** 'am, is, are'. And if the consonants **g, m, p** or **r** come between the **s** and a vowel, the **s** is not sounded **sh** even if the vowel is slender. So **sgìth** 'tired' is pronounced *skee*, **smior** 'marrow' is *smir*, **spèis** 'affection' is *spaysh*, and **sreath** 'series' is *sre*. If the consonants are **l, n,** and **t**, however, the slender vowel usually has its normal effect, so **slige** 'shell' is pronounced *shleekə*, **sneachda** 'snow' is *shnyachkə* (**ch** as in lo**ch**), and **stiall** 'stripe' is *shtyeeəl*.

Modern words borrowed from English tend to keep the English **s** sounds, so in **seusan** 'season' both instances of **s** have untraditional Gaelic sounds; the first is not an English **sh** (which might have been expected because of the **e** next to it) and the second **s** is for many speakers a **z** sound. So **seusan** sounds like *sayzen*.

Lenited **s** (**sh**) drops the **s** sound, so **sheas** 'stood' is pronounced a bit like *hess*. This is why **Eilean Shannda** (Sand Island) just off the west coast of Sutherland is Handa in English, and **Machaire Shanais** (Machair; Sanas unexplained) in Kintyre is Machrihanish. Many readers will also be familiar with Para Handy, a character in Neil Munro's tales of the puffer *The Vital Spark*. In Gaelic this would be **Para Shandaidh** (Peter son of Sandy). Lenited **s** also explains the name Hamish, which is **Sheumais** in Gaelic. In Gaelic, however, this form (with the **h** and the **i**) of **Seumas** (James) is used only when addressing someone directly (the vocative case) and so its use in English is incorrect. But Hamish has by now become an accepted name in English, joining St Kilda, Iona, Hebrides, the Grampians, Lake of Menteith, the Black Isle and Cedric (Sir Walter Scott again!) etc. as incorrect, but now established, forms based on a misunderstanding. **Mhàiri**, the vocative of **Màiri**, is showing a similar tendency.

In fairness it should be mentioned that Gaelic is just as capable of misunderstanding English. The country's most famous street, Princes Street in Edinburgh, is frequently translated wrongly as **Sràid a' Phrionnsa**, as if it were Prince's Street. Since the name refers to two princes (the Prince of Wales and the Duke of York, sons of George III), correct Gaelic would be **Sràid nam Prionnsachan**.

S is not lenited in sound before the letters **b,g,m,p** and **t**, simply because it's too difficult to say. So **sgrìobh** (*skreev*) is both *write* and *wrote*. But the **h** appears before **l**, **n**, and **r** though it's not always pronounced; so **snàmh** (*snaav*) 'swim', **shnàmh** (*hnaav* or *naav*) 'swam'.

This change of an **s** to an **h** sound is also found in English as *semi-* and *hemi-*, both meaning *half*, *sept-* and *hept-*, both meaning *seven*, and so on. It is also a feature of Welsh; Gaelic **salann** 'salt' (English *saline*) is Welsh *halen*, and the Severn is *Hafren*.

There is another occasion when **s** isn't sounded at the start of a word. This is when the word comes with the definite article (*the* in English, **an** etc. in Gaelic). It depends on the case and gender of the noun and grammar books will give the details. An example is **an t-sùil** 'the eye' which is pronounced *m tool*. This is why the surnames **Mac an t-Saoir** 'son of the joiner' is MacIntyre in English, and **Mac an t-Sagairt** 'son of the priest' is MacTaggart. In the same way the place-name **Tom an t-Sabhail** 'hillock of the barn' is Tomintoul (for the silent **bh** see under **B**) in English and **An t-Sròn** 'the promontory' is Troon.

S, like **d** and **t**, is lenited after **cha** 'not' (**ch** as in lo**ch**) in some areas but not in others, so, for instance, both **cha sheas** and **cha seas** 'will not stand' are found.

Gaelic sometimes adds an unnecessary **s** at the start of a word before another consonant. This unusual feature is the opposite of French, which frequently removes such an initial **s**, putting an **é** in its place, so that *école* is 'school', *Écosse* is 'Scotland' and so on.[1] The fact that the **s** does not belong to

---

1. This French dislike of a word starting with **s** followed by certain consonants can be seen in English too. The

the word in Gaelic can be seen from English cognates. So **smugaid** 'spit, spittle', cognate *mucus*; **sprèidh** 'cattle' cognate *predatory*, ie cattle as booty; **snèap** 'turnip', cognate *neep*; **sgudal** 'trash, offal', cognate *guts*. This addition (or removal) of initial **s** is also a feature of English, as *lash/slash, quash/squash, tummy/stomach* etc. and it continues today, as *trimmer/strimmer*.

Conversely, an initial **s** sometimes disappears, as **pòsta** 'married' (English cognate *spouse*) and **pòr** 'seed' (English cognate *spore*). So initial **s** immediately before a consonant can have a rather unsettled existence in Gaelic, particularly in dialect forms, as **(s)leamhnagan** 'stye' (in the eye), **(s)màg** 'a paw'.

S too can have a schwa, the neutral unstressed vowel, after it, when followed by **ch**. So **Glaschu** (Glasgow) is pronounced *Glassəcho* (**ch** as in lo**ch**) by many speakers.

English town of Nottingham originally began with **s** (eg Snotingeham in the Domesday Book of 1089), but lost the **s** due to Norman-French influence. And Trafford (Manchester) was originally Stratford.

T

Teine – Furze, gorse, whin
The modern word is **Conasg**.

T with a broad vowel at the start of a word is much like an English **t**, so **tana** 'thin', **tog** (*toke*) 'lift, build', **tuath** (*tooə*) 'north'. At the end of a word, or inside a word if the vowel before it doesn't have an accent, the **t** usually has a slight breathing before it; so **cat** 'cat' sounds like *caht*, and **bata** 'a stick' like *bahta*. **C** and **P** are similarly treated, as noted under these letters.

With a slender vowel, **t** sounds like **t** in English *Tuesday*, or a **tch** sound as in *church*. So **tìr** 'land' is pronounced *tcheer*, and **teas** 'heat' is pronounced *tchess*. This happens in the middle or at the end of words too, so **cait** 'cats' sounds like *catch* or, sometimes, *ketch*. So the village of (**An**) **Teallach** (forge, anvil) near Newton Stewart is *Challoch* in English, and **Teàrlach** is the Gaelic form of *Charles*. With modern words borrowed from English, however, this frequently doesn't happen (as with **d** – see under **D**). So **telebhisean** (television) begins with a hard **t** as in the English word, as does **tiogaid** (ticket).

At the beginning of a word, lenited **t** (**th**) has an **h** sound as in English *hot*, so **tha**, 'am, is, are', probably the most common Gaelic word, is pronounced *ha*. A very common exception to this is **thu** 'you' (singular) which is pronounced *oo*. As noted earlier, a lenited **s** also has this **h** sound (see

50

under **S**), so **thèid** 'will go' and **shèid** 'blew' sound roughly alike, but the context usually resolves any confusion. At the end of a word **th** is silent, as **math** 'good', pronounced *ma* (with a short **a**). So **Dùn Rath** (hill fort) – in Caithness – is in English Dounreay, and **Damh-ath** (stag ford) in Inverness-shire is Dava. Inside a word **th** may have an **h** sound; **mathanas** 'pardon, forgiveness' sounds like *mahanas*. Or it may be silent; **dùthaich** 'country' sounds like *doo-eech* (**ch** as in lo**ch**). And like other letters noted earlier, **th** can be used to separate vowels without having any etymological connection with a word; **sutha** is a Gaelic form of English *zoo*.

Like **s**, as noted above, **t** is sometimes not lenited after **cha** 'not'. The well-known song **Cha Till MacCruimein** 'MacCrimmon will not return' represents a Skye (and elsewhere) form (the MacCrimmons were a Skye clan), and the pronunciation would be *cha tcheel*. In Lewis, however, the **t** would usually be lenited, ie **cha thill** (*cha heel*).

Another feature of Lewis Gaelic (as noted also under **D**) is the disappearance of a **t** sound after **an**, both as a sign of the future tense and as the definite article. So for the former, in the well-known song **An Tèid thu leam, a Mhàiri**? 'Will you go with me, Mairi?', a Lewis singer would be likely to pronounce the first two words something like *ən yaytch* or *ən haytch*. This disappearance of the sound of **t** after **n** is, of course, common in English, as *wannabe* for *want to be*, or *twenty* as it is usually pronounced in America. It is also a feature of Welsh (the nasal mutation); 'in Tonypandy' is *yn Nhonypandy*. For the definite article, where masculine nouns have a **t** as part of the article, eg **an t-eilean** 'the island', Lewis speakers routinely say **an eilean**.

Th is never sounded as in English, though, as noted under **R**, a final **r** can sometimes have a voiced **th** sound. So modern

Gaelic words borrowed from English will not reproduce the **th** of English; thus **clò** 'clo*th*' – **Clò Hearach** is Harris Tweed. But although it's not a Gaelic sound, it occurs elsewhere in the Celtic language family; Welsh has both the voiced (written **dd**) and the unvoiced (written **th**) versions.

For the recent replacement of **d** by **t** when after **s** – eg **pòsta** 'married' instead of **pòsda** – see under **D**, and for **tn** sounded as **tr** see under **N**.

A

Ailm – Elm
The modern word is **Leamhan**.

A broad vowel. All of the vowels in Gaelic can be short or long, and it is easy to tell them apart due to the presence or absence of an accent. Long vowels have an accent over them, short vowels don't. The accent used is now generally a grave ˋ, but the acute ´ is sometimes still used. Their usage will be explained as each vowel is discussed. As far as **a** is concerned, the long sound will be represented by **à** (**à** as in *halve*) but **á** can still be found in the words **á** and **ás**, both meaning 'from', though this is no longer recommended. So **bàn** (*baan*) 'white, fair'; **An Càrn Bàn** 'The White Cairn' is rendered *Cairnbaan* in English, with the double **a** representing the long vowel sound. (This hasn't happened with **càrn**, possibly because in English *baan* takes the stress of the word.) Double vowels are not found in Gaelic, but they are a common way of showing a long vowel sound in languages which do not use an accent for this purpose; so Gaelic **bàta** (boat) is Manx *baatey*, German *boot*.

The accent also indicates stress, and since the stress in Gaelic comes on the first syllable of a word, that is where the accent, if required, will be. In words borrowed from other languages, however, it can appear on other syllables to indicate the stress; so **cangarù** 'kangaroo', **buntàta** 'potato'.

In written Gaelic the accent helps to distinguish words

which are otherwise spelled the same, as **cas** (**a** as in h**a**t) 'foot, leg' and **càs** 'difficulty, strait' – a longer sound for the latter. There are many instances of this in Gaelic, so it is important to be aware of the accent; it is frequently omitted in English language publications quoting Gaelic, though they usually manage to put accents (not always correctly) on any French quotations. It's the opposite, in a sense, of their eagerness to insert the letter **h** unnecessarily and ungrammatically, as mentioned under **H**.

Sometimes the same word may be found both with and without an accent, depending on its case or number; some common instances are **ubhal** 'apple' but **ùbhlan** 'apples', **cnò** 'nut' but **cnothan** 'nuts', **caraid** 'friend' but **càirdean** 'friends', **cù** 'dog' but **coin** 'dogs', **fiadh** 'deer' but **fèidh** 'deer' (plural), **grian** 'sun' but **grèine** 'of (the) sun' and so on.

A short **a** before **dh** and **gh** has an indeterminate sound indicated by the schwa, as **achadh** (*achəgh* –**ch** as in lo**ch**) 'field' and **tagh** (*təgh*) 'choose'. **A** is often found with this schwa sound in unstressed syllables since it now replaces the letter **u** in such positions, eg **botal** 'bottle' is now preferred to **botul**, but the latter will often be found in older books; **agus** 'and' is an exception because of its long-standing familiarity. This weak schwa *ə* is also found in the plural ending –**an**, as **clachan** (*clachən* – **ch** as in lo**ch**) 'stones'. This is one way of distinguishing in sound, if not in print, other -**an** endings (diminutives etc.) which are not plurals, as **clachan** 'a village', where the second **a** has a more distinct sound, ie both the instances of **a** in this word sound much the same.

A very short **a** sound (a schwa, really) is found in the definite article (*the*) forms **a'**, **an**, **nan** etc. Non-Gaelic speakers generally over-emphasise these words, so that their pronunciation of, for instance, **an Tairbeart** (Tarbert) sounds like a person (Anne Tarbert) rather than *'n terebərst*, and **Rèidio nan Gàidheal** (Radio of the Gaels) sounds like another person (Radio Nan Gale) rather than *Radio nən Gale*.

The *ow* (as in n*ow*) sound of **a** before **ll** and **nn** has already been mentioned – see under **L** and **N**.

The combination **ai** is very common in Gaelic and has several sounds, so here are some examples.

a) an *e* sound as in *yes*. So **aig** (*ek*) 'at', **aimsir** (*emeshir*) 'weather';

b) an *i* sound as in *by*. So **taigh** (*tie*) 'house', **faigh** (*fie*) 'get';

c) an *eh* sound as in *air*. So **air** 'on';

d) an *a* sound as in *hat*. So **mair** (*mar* – short **a**) 'last, endure';

e) a weak *i* sound (English *it*) as in the vocative **a Dhòmhnaill** (*ə ghaw-il*) 'Donald'. The insertion of the **i** is a requirement of the vocative case here; a **u** used to be written instead of the **a** in this unstressed final position, and will be found in older books, but the use of **a** is now recommended (see also under **U**).

There are other subtle distinctions, but these are the main ones. The pronunciation also depends on the area of the country and it has sometimes been difficult to give just one sound. **Taigh** 'house' mentioned above is a case in point. It is common in placenames, but its Anglicised form has several different spellings, viz **Ty**ndrum (Argyll), **Tigh**nabruaich (Argyll), **Tay**nuilt (Argyll), **Te**aninich (Ross & Cromarty). Anything but **taigh**!

The combination **ao** has a sound not found in English. So

saor 'joiner' sounds a bit like French *soeur*, and German **ö** as in *Töne* is also close to it. Because it is not an English sound it is not surprising that it has several forms in Anglicised Highland placenames. **Caol** 'narrow, a strait' is found in the following forms – **Kyle** (Lochalsh), **Col**intraive (Argyll), **Caol** (Lochaber), Balla**chul**ish (Loch Leven), **Kel**man Hill (Aberdeenshire), **Kil**churn (Loch Awe, Argyll), Eddra**chill**is (Sutherland). Not only that, Ballachulish was spelled Balle**chel**es in the 16th century, and Kilchurn was **Cheul**chern in the 18th century. Much of this has to do with the whims of non-Gaelic-speaking scribes but it does indicate that the pronunciation of **ao** can differ slightly in various parts of the country, as is still the case.

Ao also acts as a negative prefix, like English un-, in- etc., as **aotrom** 'not heavy, light' mentioned above. Some other common negative prefixes are **eas-**, **an-**, **eu-**, **mi-**, **neo-**.

With the accent, the combination **ài** sometimes has just the long **a** sound, as **Màiri** 'Mairi', **càise** (*caashə*) 'cheese'; in the latter the **i** (and the **e**) is there to affect the consonant, so that the **s** has a **sh** sound – see under **S**. This feature of the slender vowels accounts for many instances of **ài**. Or sometimes there is a long sound as in *bye*; so **làimh** (*lyve*) 'of a hand'.

The combination **aoi** is also found, as **aois** 'age' (roughly *oeush*), where the **i** is there to give the **s** a **sh** sound, which *aos* wouldn't do. There are many instances like this, but sometimes the **i** is sounded, as **caoidh** 'lament' (roughly *coeui*), **a-raoir** 'last night' (roughly *ə roeuir*).

E

Eadha – Aspen
The modern word is **Critheann**.

A slender or narrow vowel. Although an **e** by itself is often found at the end of a word, an **e** seldom stands alone before or between consonants in Gaelic; the few instances include **e** (**e** as in *set*) 'he, him, it'; **ged** 'although'; **teth** (*tchay*) 'hot'; **leth** (*lyay*) 'half'. So although the placename *Brechin*, for instance, would not offend against the spelling rule, Gaelic prefers the form *Breichin*. As a result, **e** usually stands next to another vowel and the combinations found are **ea**, **ei**, **eo**, **eu**, **eoi** and **èa**, **èi**, **eòi**, each of which will now be considered.

Ea frequently has the sound of **e**, ie the **a** is not pronounced; so **bean** (*ben*) 'woman, wife', **sean** (*shen*) 'old'. That's why **Bun Easain** (in Mull), for example, (the foot of the little waterfall) appears as Bunessan, without the first **a**, in English, and **beag** 'small' becomes the surname Begg. The **a** frequently has a purpose, of course; in **easain** it prevents the **s** from sounding **sh** – see under S. Some speakers pronounce this **ea** as a more closed **e**, so that **teas** 'heat', for example, sounds like *chase*. This is particularly the case when **ea** comes before an **s**. Sometimes, however, especially if the letters **l** or **r** are involved, **ea** is sounded with an emphasis on the **a,** as **bealach** (*byaloch*) 'a pass', **feàrna** (*fyarna*) 'alder'; so **Bealach** at the south end of Loch Lomond appears in English as Balloch, without the **e.**[1]

If **ea** does not carry the stress in a word, it often has the neutral schwa sound, as **nighean** (*nyee-ən*) 'girl, daughter'. This weak sound is also heard in the common plural ending –**ean,** as **sùilean** (*soolən*) 'eyes'.

Common words which have a different sound to **ea** are **leabhar** (*lyaw-ər*) 'book' and **teaghlach** (*tchowləch* – second **ch** as in lo**ch**) 'family'. For the *yow* sound of **ea** before **ll** and **nn,** eg **geall** (*gyowl*) 'bet' as opposed to **geal** (*gyal*) 'white', see under **L** and **N.**

Ei generally has a sound like that in *say,* as **reic** (*raychk*) 'sell', **eile** (*ehlə*) 'other', **leis** (*laysh*) 'with'. The **i** does not have a separate sound of its own, but does, of course, exert an influence on the consonant next to it – **leis,** for instance, has its **s** softened to **sh** (see under **S**). So in the placename **Geiseadar** (Goat Farmstead) in Lewis the **i** is not required in the English Geshader.

Eo has a sound like that in *yaw,* with the **o** predominant.

---

1. The forms Belloch and Bellochantuy (**Bealach an t-Suidhe**) 'the pass of the seat' (both in Kintyre) may represent an earlier pronunciation; both **e** and **a** are heard in the two different modern pronunciations. **Bealach** was *belach* in Old Irish and Kintyre Gaelic had an Irish flavour, though **bealach** was pronounced there in the normal way, ie with emphasis on the **a,** by the time Gaelic died out in Kintyre around the middle of the last century. The Loch Lomond Balloch was written Belloch in earlier centuries as was Ballochandrain in Cowal, but confusingly, the Kintyre Bellochs appear as Ballochs in Blaeu's atlas featuring Pont's maps of the late sixteenth century.

So **deoch** (*dyoch* – **ch** as in lo**ch**) 'a drink', **neoni** (*nyonee*) 'nothing', **seo** (*sho*) 'this'. So **Ciseorn** (near Lochcarron) is in English Kishorn without the **e**. Again the **e** affects the sound of the adjacent consonants.

Eu has a single sound like that in *say* (like **ei** above), as **feum** (*fame*) 'need', **ceum** (*came*) 'step, degree'. There is no separate **u** sound, and transliterated placenames generally use only an **e**, as **Geusto**, English Gesto, in Skye. More frequently, however, **eu** is pronounced **ia** with two sounds; so **feur** 'grass' sounds like *fiar*, **sgeul** 'story' like *skial* and so on. This is the pronunciation of the majority of speakers, but in Argyll the single sound of **eu** is still heard; **Beul an Atha** (The Mouth of the Ford – in English Bridgend) in Islay is pronounced locally *Bale n-e* (second **e** as in *wet*). Interestingly **ia** is now written instead of **eu** in the word **ciad** 'first', to distinguish it from **ceud** 'hundred', but both words have the same pronunciation.

E can also have an accent over it, to give a long sound. Both the grave and the acute accent used to be employed, and they gave the **e** sounds similar to French *père* and *Écosse*, ie the sounds in English *let* and *lay* respectively. This could be quite handy since it distinguished the pronunciation of **glé** (*glay*) 'very' from **cè** (**e** as in *let*) 'cream'. Since there were very few words with this open **e** (*let*) sound, it is now recommended that only one accent, the grave, be used (with all vowels), so **glé** is now **glè**, but still pronounced *glay*. This change has been widely, but not universally, accepted.

Accented combinations of **e** and another vowel are **èa** and **èi**, as well as **eò** where the accent is on the **o**. **Èa** is quite rare; **dèan** 'make, do' is the only really common instance and, as the accent indicates, the **è** gets the emphasis; *jee-an* is the usual pronunciation. **Èi** is common, and sometimes both vowels are heard, with more stress on the **è**, as **fèidh** (*fayee*) 'deer'. Sometimes, however, the **i** isn't heard, as **èist** (*aystch*) 'listen', **fèis** (*faysh*) 'festival'. **Eò** is also found, and the stress is on the **ò**; so **beò** (*byaw* or *beaw*) '(a)live', **ceòl** (*kyawl* or *keawl*) 'music'.

Also found is the combination **eòi**, as in **beòil** (*byaw-il*) 'of a mouth', **geòidh** (*gyawee*) 'geese', where the stress is on the **ò** and the other two vowels are very lightly sounded. This is the only permitted combination of three vowels starting with **e**. This means that when the common suffix **–ach** ('pertaining to, belonging to', as **Ìleach** 'belonging to Islay') is added to a word such as **ceò** 'smoke, mist', *ceòach* is not allowed; instead, **th** is inserted to separate the consonants, so we find **ceò*th*ach** 'smoky, misty'. As mentioned earlier, Gaelic frequently inserts a lenited consonant into a word to separate vowels, and this lenited consonant is not pronounced nor, as in **ceòthach**, has it any etymological connection with the word.

I

Iogh – Yew
The modern word is **Iubhar**.

A slender or narrow vowel. It is found by itself in words such
as **fir** (*feer*) 'men', **ris** (*reesh*) 'to' etc. It also has a weaker sound,
like the **i** in *bit*, so **gin** (**g** hard) 'anything', **sin** (*shin*) 'that'. In
monosyllables before **nn** it sometimes has the vowel sound in
English *time*; so **rinn** (*rine*) 'made, did', **binn** (*bine*) 'melodious',
and this sound is also heard before **nn** when a **u** precedes the
i, as in **cruinn** 'round'. This isn't always the case, though;
linne 'pool' sounds more like *leen-yə*.

Gaelic also uses the combinations **ia**, **io** and **iu**. Both vowels
are sounded in the **ia** group, as **siar** (*sheear*) 'west', though
the emphasis is on the **i**. In the combination **io** both vowels
can be heard, as **sìos** (*sheeəs*) 'down'. Often, however, the **o**
has no sound of its own, as **tioram** (*tcheerəm*) 'dry', **fios** (*feess*)
'knowledge'. The **o** does have a purpose, though, since it
affects the adjacent consonant – **fios**, for instance, if written
fis, would be pronounced *feesh*, which is not the required
sound. The combination **iu** has the stress on the **u**, with the **i**
sounding rather like an initial **y** in English. So **iuchair** (*yoochir*
– **ch** as in lo**ch**) 'key', **siubhail** (*shyoo-il*) 'travel'.

A grave accent can also be placed over **i** to give a long
vowel sound, as **cìr** (*keer*) 'comb', **mìn** (*meen*) 'smooth'. In
placenames **ì** is often represented by **ee** in English, as
Achnasheen for **Ach(adh) na Sìne** (Field of the storm). The

62

accent also appears in the combination **ìo**, and again, both vowels can be heard, though the stress is, of course, on the **ì**. So **crìoch** (*kreeəch* – **ch** as in lo**ch**) 'end, boundary', **fìon** (*feeən*) 'wine'. But often the **o** has no sound, as **cìobair** (*keeper* – **ee** long) 'shepherd'.

This is the only combination found with **ì**, and it never has a vowel immediately before it, ie the combinations **aì**, **eì**, **oì** and **uì** are not found. This presumably explains the spelling of the common name **Catrìona** (Catherine), a spelling which goes against the Gaelic spelling rule (see the introduction). An alternative spelling **Caitrìona** – found, for instance, in the placename St Catherines (**Cill Chaitrìona**) in Cowal, Argyll – conforms to the rule. It does suggest however, that the **t** may have a *tch* sound (see under T), although the combination **tr** always features a hard **t** even when followed by a slender vowel, as **trì** 'three'. So **Catrìona** is probably the best option, since the **t** is always sounded hard. There are certainly other occasional exceptions to the spelling rule – notably past participles and words borrowed from other languages – and the Gaelic spelling of some other names disregards the traditional **t** sound, as **Ceit** 'Kate'.

The combination **iùi**, with the accent on the **ù**, is also found. The stress is, of course, on the **ù**, and the first **i** has a sound, but the second **i** hardly does. So **siùil** (*shyool*) 'sails', **ciùin** (*kyoon*) 'gentle'. But, as ever, the second **i** makes its presence felt; the **l** in **seòl** (*shyawl*) 'a sail' has a different sound in Gaelic from the **l** in the plural **siùil**. (See under **L**.)

O

Oir – the Spindle Tree
Also known as **Feòras**.

A broad vowel. It has two sounds in Gaelic, an open one (like English *for*) and a closed one (like English (*fore*). It is often possible to distinguish between them in English by the spelling, a final **e** being a good clue, as with *fore*. Other alphabets, eg Greek, had two different letters for the separate sounds.

Things are not so easy in Gaelic. **Robh** 'was, were' and **crodh** 'cattle' have the closed **o**, so sound like *roe* and *crow* respectively. But the open **o** is heard in **dol** 'going', which sounds like *doll* (with a shorter **o**) and **dona** 'bad', which sounds like the female name Donna. It is probably safest just to learn the sound of each word as it appears, rather than try to explain why, for instance, **tog** 'lift' is pronounced *toke*, but **snog** 'nice' is pronounced *snock* (**o** as in *rock*).

For the *ow* sound (as in *now*) of **o** before **ll**, **nn** and **m**, eg **donn** (*down*) 'brown', see under **L**, **N** and **M**.

The combination **oi** is also found. Sometimes both vowels are sounded, particularly before a lenited consonant, as **oidhche** (*oychə* – **ch** as in lo**ch**) 'night', **toigh** (*toi*) 'agreeable'. But often the **i** isn't sounded, as **loisg** (*loshk*) 'burn', **goirt** (*gorstch*) 'sore' etc. There are also a few words in which **oi** has a neutral schwa sound, as **doirbh** (*dərəv*) 'difficult', **soirbh** (*sərəv*) 'easy', **goid** (*gətch*) 'steal'.

O is also found with an accent. This was formerly used to distinguish between the open and closed sounds of the letter as described above. So **mór** 'big' is pronounced *more*, and **ròn** 'a seal' is pronounced *rawn*, and this was a helpful way for learners to get the correct sound. But, as with **e**, it is now recommended that only the grave accent be used, so **mór** is now written **mòr**, but still pronounced *more*. So now the sound of words such as **bò** and **gòrach** is not immediately obvious; it's *bow* (as in bow-tie) and *gawrəch* (**ch** as in lo**ch**). One useful pointer, however, is that Gaelic uses the open **o** in words borrowed from English, even where English has the closed sound. So **còta** (*cawtə*) is 'coat', **bòrd** (*bawrd*) is 'board, table', **stròc** (*strawchk*) is 'stroke' (cerebral). This also happens even if there is no accent on the **o**, as **post** (to rhyme with English *lost*) 'post, mail', **lof** 'a loaf '.

The combination **òi** is also found. The **o** sound, which carries the accent, predominates but there is also usually an **i** sound, as **bòidheach** (*boiyəch* – **ch** as in lo**ch**) 'pretty', **còig** (*co-ik* – **o** as in *go*) 'five'.

Sometimes, though, the **i** has no sound, as **tòiseachadh** (*tawshəchəgh* – **ch** as in lo**ch**) 'beginning', **a' mhòid** (*ə vawj*) 'of the mod'. As usual, however, the influence of the **i** can be seen in the consonants following it. (See under **S** and **D**.)

U

Ur – Heath
The modern word is **Fraoch**.

A broad vowel. Without an accent **u** has the sound of English *put, foot*. So **cus** (kooss) 'too much', **luch** (*looch* – **ch** as in lo**ch**) 'mouse'. In unstressed syllables it had a weak neutral sound indicated by the use of a schwa; so **farum** (*farəm*) 'noise'. It is now recommended, however, that **u** be replaced by **a** in such instances, so the word is now written **faram**, and the (second) **a** now has this sound. (See under **A**.)

When **u** and **ù** are followed by an **m** at the end of a word they have an *ow* (as in *now*) sound in Lewis. So **cum** 'keep' sounds like *cowm*, and **rùm** 'room' like *rowm*.

The combinations **ua** and **ui** are also found. In words with **ua** both vowels are sounded, with the emphasis on the **u**; so **fuar** (*fooər*) 'cold', **uan** (*ooan*) 'lamb'. With **ui** both vowels are also heard, again with the emphasis on the **u**, as **cluich** (**ch** as in lo**ch**) 'play', **dhuibh** (*ghuiv*) 'to you'. Often, however, the **i** sound is very faint, as in **muir** 'sea', and not really heard at all in **uisge** (*ooshkə*) 'water, rain'. In such instances, though, the presence of the **i** can be 'heard' in the adjacent consonant, as frequently mentioned above and in accordance with Gaelic spelling conventions.

Ùi, with an accent on the **ù**, is also common, as **sùil** (*sooil*) 'eye', **cùis** (*coosh*) 'matter, affair', and in such instances the **ù**

has a long stressed sound and the **i** has hardly any sound at all. The lack of an **i** sound is evident in the placename **Baile na Cùil** 'Farmstead in the Corner', which appears in Arran as Balnacoole and in Moray as Balnacoul, neither with the letter **i**.

In the combination **uai** the **u** has its normal sound and the **ai** has an **i** sound as in English *high*. So **fuaim** 'noise, sound' is pronounced something like *foo-I'm*, and **cruaidh** 'hard' like *kroo-aye*. Again, there will be cases where the **i** has less of an influence on the vowel sound, but rather has an effect on the consonant following, as **gluais** (*glooəsh*) 'move', **fhuair** (*hooer*) 'got, found'. This is a fundamental feature of Gaelic orthography.

WORD LIST

Here is a list of fifty common Gaelic words, none of which appear in the text above. Readers may wish to make an attempt at the correct pronunciation based on information given in the book. Alongside each word I have given an approximate phonetic equivalent, and you may wish to cover this up while you say the word; the phonetics can then be uncovered to confirm, or correct, your pronunciation. If you don't understand why a letter or part of a word is pronounced as indicated, you can look back under the letter(s) concerned. In the phonetic pronunciations I have used bold type to indicate the dark or back **l** (see under **L**), and the schwa (see in the Introduction) is used to indicate a neutral vowel. Remember, too, that the stress is on the first syllable of the word, and that an accent means a long vowel.

So, as an example, take **dithis**. This word means 'two persons' and will also be familiar to many pipers as a term used in **pìobaireachd** (pibroch). Its pronunciation is *jee-ish*. The stress is on the first syllable, as always in Gaelic, and the **d** has a **j** sound because of the following slender vowel (see under **D**). The first **i** has its usual *ee* sound, but the second **i** has the much weaker sound of English *is* (see under **I**). The **th** in the middle of the word isn't sounded, as frequently happens (see under **T**). And the final **s** has a **sh** sound because of the slender vowel next to it (see under **S**).

Gaelic	English	Phonetic Spelling of Gaelic
a-rithist	again	ə ree-istch
a' ghealach	the moon	ə yalləch (ch as in *loch*)
aibidil	alphabet	apitchil
airgead	silver, money	erekət
am measg	among	ə -mesk
an t-slat	the rod	ən tlaht
banais	wedding	banish
Beurla	English lang.	bayərlə
cadal	sleep	katəl
caidil	sleep!	katchil
cearc	hen	kerk
còmhradh	conversation	cawragh
creideamh	belief	kraytchəv
crios	a belt	creess
cuidich	help!	kootcheech (2nd ch as in *loch*)
cumhachd	power	koo-achk (ch as in *loch*)
dath	a colour	dah
dealbh	a picture	jyalav
deiseil	ready	jayshel
dh'fhàs	grew, became	ghaas
dhìrich	climbed	yeereech (ch as in *loch*)
dia	god	jee-ə

Gaelic	English	Phonetic Spelling of Gaelic
eaglais	church	eklish
earball	a tail	erəpəl
fosgladh	opening	fosgləgh
gheibh	will get	yave
gann	scarce	gown
idir	at all	eetchir
lorg	trace, track	lawrok
maide	a stick	matchə
màileid	a bag	maaletch
neòil	clouds	nyawil
nochd	appear	nawchk (ch as in *loch*)
Peairt	Perth	Pyarstch
piseag	kitten	peeshak
rìgh	king	ree
ro fhaisg	too close	roe ashk
sàmhach	quiet	saavəch (ch as in *loch*)
searbh	bitter	sharav
sheòl	sailed	hyawl
shuidh	sat	hooee
sìde	weather	sheetchə
slighe	way, path	shlee-ə
tapadh leat	thank you	tahpə lat

Gaelic	English	Phonetic Spelling of Gaelic
teann	tight	tchown (ow as in *now*)
theab	almost	hape
thuit	fell	hootch
tilg	throw	tcheelik
treas	third	tress
uiseag	a lark	ooshak

Finally, ten words chosen at random from the large (and increasing) number of English words in Gaelic dress found in print today; such words are a good illustration of Gaelic spelling rules put into practice.

air loidhne	on line
bhìoto	veto
ciudha	queue
daithead	diet
mions	mince
paidse	patch
poidsear	poacher
pròiseact	project
seanal	channel
siostam	system

Such words become easier to recognise once you've got used to the traditional Gaelic spelling system, though, as mentioned before, modern words are sometimes not written completely in accordance with the spelling rules. Thus the initial **s** of **siostam** is an English, not a Gaelic **s** sound (see under **S**) and **paidse** might well be written **paide** or **paite**, but **ds** is commonly used in such instances (**frids** = fridge, **loidsig** = logic, and so on) following the spelling of other words borrowed from English centuries ago, as **buidseach** from English *witch*.

Other Books from Argyll Publishing

Scots Gaelic – a brief introduction
George McLennan
ISBN:1 902831 88 8 £4.99 paperback 80pages
In contrast to native speakers, who absorb the language as
children, adults who are learning Gaelic from scratch often
derive much benefit from knowing *why* the language takes
shape as it does. This bestselling Gaelic primer keeps things
as simple as possible to accommodate readers who may be
taking a first look at the language, but those whose knowledge
of Gaelic is a little more advanced also find the book useful.

The Skye Bridge Story
– multi-national interests and people power
compiled by **Andy Anderson**
ISBN: 978 1 906134 19 8 £14.99 hardback 256pages
Richly illustrated and presented as a complete bilingual
Gaelic/English text, The Skye Bridge Story is a life-affirming
account of what is possible when people exercise their sense
of justice. Andy Anderson was a Skye Bridge campaigner who
was charged and was remanded in prison for refusal to pay
the tolls. He has been assisted by numerous local people in
the compilation of this book.

Available from your usual outlets and direct from Argyll Publishing
www.argyllpublishing.com